Author
Dr. Lisa N. Folden
Blue Topaz Publishing

©2018 Dr. Lisa Folden
Blue Topaz Publishing
Design by Twenty One Design and Promotions
Written by Dr. Lisa Folden
Photos supplied by www.pexels.com and Dr. Lisa Folden

Dr. Lisa Folden is a licensed physical therapist in North Carolina. The advice and strategies suggested in this work may not be suitable for every situation. This work is sold with the understanding that neither the author nor the publisher are held responsible for results accrued from the advice within this book.

All rights reserved. No part of this book may be reproduced in any form or by any electronic and mechanical means (except in the case of quotations with credit given) without written permission from its publisher and author.

Printed in the United States of America
ISBN #:978-1-7325476-1-2

Table of Contents

Dedication

Preface

Intro: Where Do I Start?

Part One: Food

Chapter 1: How to Plan, Schedule and Prepare Healthy Meals

Chapter 2: How to Appease Your Kids and Family While Transitioning to a Healther Diet

Chapter 3: How to Enjoy Social Eating Without Feeling Like An Outcast

Part Two: Exercise

Chapter 4: How to Plan, Prepare and Schedule Workouts

Chapter 5: How To Incorporate Kids Into Your Workout Routine

Chapter 6: How To Plan A workout at the Playground

Chapter 7: How to Incorporate Fitness into Your Family Life/Activities

Chapter 8: How to Navigate the Equipment at the Gym for an Effective Workout

Chapter 9: How to Design a Workout Without Equipment

Chapter 10: How to Focus on Your Fitness without the Weight of Comparison

About the Author

Dedication

This book is dedicated to my "G-Lady," Olivia Hilmon. The woman who taught me the importance of preparing for things in advance. The hardest working and most kind woman I have ever known. I sincerely hope that you are proud of me and I miss you more than I could ever
explain.

This book is also dedicated to my Tribe of supporters that cover me daily with so much love, encouragement and inspiration. The list is far too long to write, but you ALL know who you are.

Preface

With all of the responsibility that rests on women, one might think that being healthy would automatically be easy. We are running companies, organizing households, teaching and training children (ours and everyone else's), cooking, cleaning, loving, caregiving, volunteering and the list most certainly goes on. We fight in wars, birth children, preside over courtrooms, break up fights in high schools, run state governments, host dinner parties and all the while, we STILL have to make time for own fitness. Seriously, you would think we could expect healthy food to be on our doorstep every morning and we would each have a gym clone who spent the day running and lifting weights in a lab so that we could reap the benefits of health without disturbing our daily routine. Alas, no such luck. So, as with most things, it is up to us. We have to take control. We have to MAKE the time that does not exist. We have to multitask and work it out. We have to use our resources and creative juices to produce what can be called nothing else, other than MAGIC. We do it every day, though seldom acknowledged. And it is magic. So, let us start there. Right there...with the knowing that whatever you have been able to accomplish up until this point is MAGIC... amazing and noteworthy. You may be reading this in an effort to "better yourself" or get your "life together," but please let me remind you of all that you have already done. You are doing just fine. Tips, tricks and tools may help you to be more efficient and maybe more successful in the eyes of others, but remember to always be mindful of the effort you have always brought to the table and know that your worth as a woman far exceeds the benefits of seemingly "having it all together." So let's talk about ways to enhance who you already are as it relates to managing your fitness and family, because after all, healthy really should be easy.

Intro: Where Do I Start?

As with any project (and yes, this lifestyle change will be a project, constantly changed and tweaked to meet fluctuating demands and desires), we must begin with a plan. I encourage clients to utilize a paper planner (yes, old school) and write down your plans, goals, activities and assignments.

I strongly suggest the Empowered Planner by Nedra Tawwab. This planner is all about writing your vision and making it plain. With sections for yearly/monthly/weekly planning, you'll be prompted to set realistic and feasible goals. Snag this stylish planner at www.nedratawwab.com

Begin with your yearly and monthly views. Decide right away on the number and frequency of family trips you would like to take and determine a month for each. I like to plan one family trip away (more than three hrs), one local family trip (less than three hrs) and one trip with just my husband and I. I also like to try to squeeze in a girls trip for myself and occasionally my husband will plan one for himself as well. When prioritizing the needs of yourself and your family, I find it therapeutic to begin with the fun stuff first. Looking ahead to trips and outings can help make planning for the more tedious activities less stressful.

Once the trips are at least tentatively scheduled, come up with a list of local, kid-centered/friendly family activities that would interest you, your spouse and your children. As manager of the household, I would suggest making executive decisions on these items. You probably know your family well enough to pick for them, but if you really want them to be involved, feel free to take a family vote on multiple activities and assign the top twelve to one month each of the year. Most importantly, make sure that 1/3 to 1/2 of the activities are ACTIVE (we will talk about this more later).

Lastly, look over you and your spouse's calendars (work and personal) as well as your children's school and extra-curricular activity calendars. Eliminate activities that overlap, consider potential chaperoning responsibilities for field trips (if that is something that you do) and try as best as you can to organize plans for the course of the year. Do not stress over this part because things will inevitably change, but by having a "skeleton plan" in place, coming up with ideas and activities will be much less taxing on a monthly or quarterly basis.

Once the calendar is set in what I like to call "tentative mode," you can move on to planning the daily and weekly aspects of your life related to physical health and wellness. This is where you will decide on your workout days and times and your meal planning agenda.

Part One: Food

Chapter 1: How to Plan, Schedule and Prepare Healthy Meals

Now that you have a good idea of what your year will look like as it relates to travel and activities, let's figure out one of the most important components to our health...FOOD. Another reason I suggest the *Empowered Planner* by Nedra Tawwab, is because it includes weekly meal planning sections for this exact purpose.

I often start more broad, planning for the entire month by making a list of four breakfast options, 4-8 lunch options (depending on whether these are different or the same for children and adults) and twelve dinners. This can seem a bit overwhelming (if so, by all means revert to a mini-version that you manage weekly), but I have come to enjoy this method because it makes weekly grocery lists and shopping a BREEZE. By deciding ahead of time what foods my family and I will be eating for the month, I can group items with similar ingredients together. Utilizing this simple tip helps to keep our grocery bill low each week and also keeps us from wasting as much food.

I use multiple sources for food inspiration. The internet is full of great options. Here are a few of my favorite Instagram accounts for meal planning tips and recipe ideas. If these pages don't get you inspired, I have no idea what will.
@cafedelights
@tasteofhome
@feelgoodfoodie
@mealprep.andchill
@cleanfoodcrush
@cookinglight

You may have noticed that utilizing this meal planning format means repeated meals during the week. For example, week one, you will eat the same breakfast each day, the same lunch each day and you will have three dinner options, either to choose from daily, or as I prefer, to eat on for two days consecutively, each. Subscribing to the latter method, leaves you 1-2 days available for additional leftovers, dinner out or some carry-out. Therefore, you are planning with contingencies in place for when the plan does not go as planned. If you live in my house, this happens often, but all is well. If you are not a leftover kind of person, I assume that meal prepping is not going to work for you in any form. Hopefully, though, you have the type of life and schedule that will allow you to cook and prep on a daily basis. If that works for you, God bless you and keep it up! That is amazing in my book...but then again, so is planning and preparing in advance. The bottom line is:

do what works best for you (first) and your family (second). As house manager, you must be pleased with the process most of all because you are the one carrying it all out. If you are fortunate enough to have some assistance with cooking and meal planning from your partner, that is awesome. You can then adopt multiple formats for your meal-planning that works for each of you. Figuring out your food for the week or month will create a new level of fluidity in your grocery list writing, shopping and preparing. I typically write my lists on Thursday evenings, right after my kids go to bed. My ideal position is cozy on the living room couch with a glass of wine beside me, the tv tuned to one of my favorite shows (the one that requires the least of my attention since I'm multitasking) and my notepad, pen and coupon books neatly arranged on my lap. I get in a zone planning meals, noting necessary ingredients (occasionally getting up from said cozy position to check cabinets and the fridge for ingredients...it's the little things) and clipping coupons that are applicable. I think it is important to note here that while I love the *idea* of coupons, I am NOT that girl. I shop at our local big box (BJ's) so I review their coupons to see what is on sale that we typically buy. I also review the ONE coupon mailer that I receive weekly. Usually, there's not much in there that applies to my family, so I spend less than 5 min/week on coupons. I do not knock those that do...I actually envy their savings abilities. However, I find that many of the items on

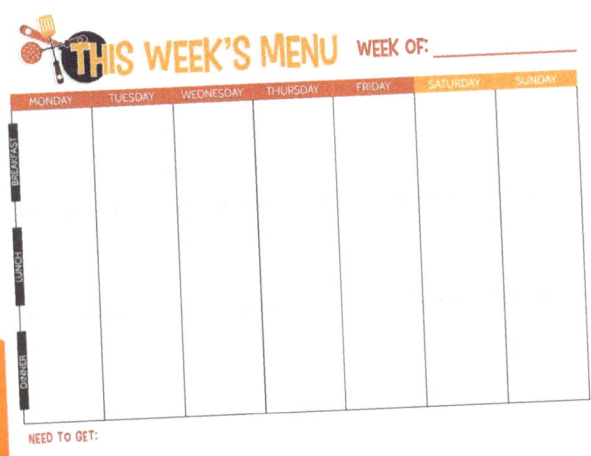

sale are pre-packaged foods, heavily containing preservatives or just not the most "healthy" or tasty to myself and my family, so it's not worth the investment of time and energy for me. I also am not the type of house manager to alter meals based on what's on sale...  although I think it is a great idea to "shop sales," I'm just a bit stubborn in that regard. I want what I want. Having said that, if you are a couponing machine, you are probably already an excellent planner, so incorporating these tips into your program will either be completely unnecessary OR absolutely life changing. I hope the latter.

Once the meals are selected, groceries are listed, coupons are clipped and you are feeling great about yourself, why not take it a step further and order your groceries online? Okay, so this may not be news to all of you, but you might be surprised at what stores and what third-party companies offer grocery delivery or curbside pick-up right in your neighborhood for a very small fee or free. Some stores offer monthly or yearly curbside or delivery prices to make grocery shopping super simple and super convenient. Now granted, I know that some of you enjoy grocery shopping or even yet, some of you utilize those steps to get in some extra activity during the day (and you might even be step champ on your Fitbit), but just know that later on, I will share some additional tips on getting in as much activity and movement as possible during your day. You will not miss out by avoiding a grocery store trip, I promise. And if you're like me, your weekly shopping consists of visiting two stores, so to have one of those stops, NOT require us to get out of the car is EVERYTHING.

Believe it or not, the hard part is done. You have created the meal options, planned for the week or month, compiled the grocery lists and shopped! Now it is time to cook. Everyone has their own method as it relates to cooking. Depending on your work schedule, you may prefer to take a few hours on Saturday or Sunday to knock everything out all at once. Or maybe you like to spread it out over the weekend or even do a few meals during the week (I suggest this option for items that will be immediately frozen). Whatever you do, as long as you have a plan that you can easily stick with, you are good to go.

I used to dedicate portions of Friday, Saturday AND occasionally Sunday to meal prep, but I've found that entirely too hard to keep up with. Instead, I assign Fridays to errands and laundry, Saturdays to cleaning and Sundays to meal prep. Sometimes I will get up early, workout and knock out the cooking right away. Other times, I will enjoy my day, go to a sorority or book club meeting and handle the cooking in the evening. I allow myself some freedom with the timing just so I do not feel completely overwhelmed. Sounds silly but over-planning, over-analyzing and forcing yourself to stick to super strict time constraints can be even more stressful than NOT planning and having to figure everything out on the fly!

Give yourself reasonable, BUT flexible, guidelines.
Also, make this process somewhat enjoyable. Set up a cooking playlist and enjoy your favorite music while in the kitchen. It will make the biggest difference. Singing and dancing along to great music is an easy way to make the time pass quickly. My meal prep usually takes about 2-3 hours. That's it. By utilizing similar ingredients and planning properly, this process can be pretty quick. Another tip for decreasing your time on meal prep is to plan 1-2 of your weekly dinners as a crockpot meal or casserole. This will work in your favor because "prepping" for these meals will not require any actual cooking...just chopping/cutting, seasoning/marinating and bagging up. This tip is really a time saver for me. With my family of five, making more than 15 individual lunches for the week in addition to breakfast and dinner can seem like a lot. By reducing the amount of work required for dinners, I can spend less time in the kitchen and more time with my family or enjoying some down time.

Meal prep can even double as a family activity. Many children LOVE to help in the kitchen, so consider this. Now, full disclosure here...I am usually on a mission and kids in my kitchen tend to slow me down. So, if they do not ask (and by ask, I mean BEG) to help, I will do it alone. However, I do often let them grab certain lunch items to fill up their containers...or from time to time, I will let them use their kid-friendly knives to chop up fruit or vegetables with me.

We love these knives for kids. They come in a set of 3 and they are super safe (so far)! Star Pack Nylon Kitchen Knife Set (3 Piece). Find them on Amazon.com

Whether you complete this process alone or with help, just appreciate that you have taken a significant step in simplifying your life. You will most definitely thank yourself later.

Chapter 2: How to Appease your Kids and Family While Transitioning to a Healthier Diet

Since you are ready to tackle meal prepping like a pro, let us discuss what types of foods you want to eat and how to deal with your pickiest little eaters. I am from an older school style of cooking/eating with kids. As a child I was pretty much told to eat what was on the plate (regardless of my personal preferences). If I did not eat, I was just going to be hungry. No one was making two dinners to appease me as a kid. And in all honesty, I somewhat agree with that idea. I have had the pleasure of having three kids that are not very picky so most of what I cook, is eaten without issue. Of course, green items are lower on the totem pole than macaroni, potatoes or chicken nuggets... but in general, they will eat fish, vegetables, beans, pasta, soup and nearly everything else. I realize that this is not always the case with children, but I do encourage people to do their very best to expand their little people's palates. It can be taxing and annoying while you are going through it, but you will have your child ready for the culinary world...open to trying new things and without a significant amount of food aversions. This will pay off when you are out to eat.

The reality is, no matter how hard you try, there are things that your kids will not like. My oldest will NOT eat tomatoes... and the first (and last) time I "forced" her, she vomited all over my kitchen floor. It serves me right I suppose but don't judge me too harshly. I thought what I was doing was the best way to elicit the response I wanted. I learned that while she loves ketchup, pizza and marinara sauce, the texture of a tomato ignited her gag reflex badly. So, no more tomatoes for her.

When a serious allergy, aversion or distaste is NOT the issue, I suggest sneaking vegetables in WHEREVER you can. I try to ensure that my kids get a small veggie serving three times each day. Our most common breakfast is egg muffins. I can hide TONS of veggies in those...tomatoes, bell peppers, onion, garlic, mushrooms, spinach and more. My kids love them...mostly because I dice the ingredients up so small that they do not even realize what they are eating. For lunch I throw in baby carrots as a side, if I do not utilize a veggie in the main dish. A good example is cheese quesadillas. I mix in some yellow bell peppers with the cheese and my kids are none the wiser! For dinner, we typically serve protein plus veggie...except 1-2 evenings per week when we order pizza, some other carryout or when I make everyone fend for themselves. PB&J anyone? If we are in the mood for pasta at dinner, I will do a vegetable-infused pasta as opposed to standard pasta. The kids certainly cannot taste the difference, so everyone is pleased. I also suggest replacing cream-based sauces for pasta with pesto or other vegetable bases. When cream is a necessity, I use plain, low fat Greek yogurt or almond milk. Again, my kids never seem to notice and always appreciate a full stomach.

Egg Muffin recipe (from 15 Days of Phitness)

RECIPE:
- *12 eggs*
- *Black Pepper*
- *1 green bell pepper*
- *1 red bell pepper*
- *5 pre-cooked chicken sausage*
- *Pre-heat oven to 350 degrees. Gently whisk eggs in large bowl. Chop bell peppers and sausage finely and add to egg bowl. Sprinkle with black pepper to taste and pour into a greased muffin pan. Fill each pan 1/2 to 3/4 full. Bake for 20 min and let cool. Store in the refrigerator in a zip lock bag for the week.*

Whatever your method, do your best to ensure that your family, especially the children, are getting as much nutrition as possible. The beauty of their baby metabolisms is that weight is rarely an issue, but remember, weight is not the only indicator of health. Over-indulging in sugar, trans fats and foods high in cholesterol can have very negative effects on adults and children...and often, these effects are not visible to the human eye.

If you have a spouse or live in partner that you prepare and cook meals for, making huge changes in your eating routine can be even more difficult. My advice is to try to get them on board from the beginning by discussing the benefits, including them in meal planning and considering their meal preferences. But if you find that method ineffective, treat them like the kids and create meals with "hidden health," or, consider preparing and cooking your meals separately. There are ways to make what you need in conjunction with what they want. Just do not overwork yourself and be sure to put your nutrition first. Work with the other important people in your life, but remember, if you are not taking care of yourself FIRST, you cannot take care of others.

Chapter 3: How to Enjoy Social Eating Without Feeling Like an Outcast

Going out to eat is by far, one of the most challenging activities to do when you're "dieting." But when you are "changing your eating habits," it does not HAVE to be. Typically, when you are trying to avoid certain foods, a social outing that includes food either goes one of two ways.

The first way, I like to call "Baby Bird Eater." The Baby Bird Eater is going to draw some unnecessary attention to themselves by reviewing the menu in great detail, checking for calories, carbs and other nutritional details. This person will ask the server tons of questions and when the complimentary bread arrives, they will announce their disinterest and turn their nose up at the rest of the table. Their entree will consist of salad and protein only. They will likely have a hunger headache and may even be excessively moody. Do not be this person. This person could potentially ruin their entire social experience by trying to stick to an eating plan that may be healthy but also unrealistic.

The second way I have observed people respond to social eating is something I like to call "Crazy Cheater Eater." The Crazy Cheater Eater has "saved" up all their calories for the week to enjoy a cheat meal (or two) during this outing. They WILL have the bread...and lots of it! They will also draw unnecessary attention to themselves by announcing that they are having a cheat meal and will hardly be able to control their excitement! The problem is, they will likely be enjoying a cheat appetizer, a cheat entree and a cheat dessert in addition to the pre-meal bread. Do not be this person either. This type of behavior inches away from "cheating" and starts to look more like BINGING. This can be extremely unhealthy and very counterproductive to your wellness goals. Overeating is never a good thing. Expanding your stomach, redefining the appetite after repeat occurrences and feeding those not-so-healthy addictions are always bad. Specifically, if you're trying to lose weight, you will find that frequent binging like this will completely sabotage your goals.

Instead of Baby Bird Eating and Crazy Cheater Eating, consider time with friends or family as an opportunity to embrace the "relaxed" version of healthy eating. Follow these tips to guarantee your success (and pleasure) during social eating:

- **Study the menu ahead of time.** If you have the privilege of knowing where you are going to eat beforehand, take a minute and review the menu online. Decide in advance what you will have and get an idea of the nutritional value in your options.

- **Set a realistic plan.** Time with your friends, family or even co-workers should be enjoyable and let's just be honest, eating delicious food is very enjoyable! So, while you are studying the menu, decide what you are willing to splurge on (if anything). For example, will you give in and have your favorite fried appetizer? Or will you opt for loaded fries as a side dish? Maybe you have been wanting a decadent dessert or a fruity high calorie drink at this particular restaurant? If you are helping to celebrate something such as a birthday, consider that there will be cake or something similar. My advice here is to pick wisely. We are trying to avoid being the Crazy Cheater Eater, right? So, pick ONE thing to splurge on. Having three calorie-rich drinks, fried macaroni and cheese and a huge piece of cake all at once is probably going to deter you from your fitness goals. Obviously, everyone is different so we all have varying triggers. Some people can spend an entire meal (or day even) eating like the Crazy Cheater Eater and make up for it over the course of the week without gaining a significant amount of weight or derailing their goals. In my experience though, those people are more of the exception and not the rule. So, following these healthy suggestions should help keep you safe.

- **Try just a taste.** Perhaps you have decided to stay strict to your eating plan during your next social outing. That is an awesome idea...especially for those of us who go out and engage in social eating on a very regular (weekly or more) basis. Or maybe you just did not have an opportunity to plan ahead by looking at a menu. Some outings will and should be spontaneous. In these cases, consider simply *tasting* things that are off of your eating plan. For example, if you are enjoying family style dining, cut yourself a quarter of a cookie or a sliver of cake...or maybe a teaspoon of loaded mashed potatoes. Or, if you are dining with close friends or family that have ordered something your taste buds are screaming for, ask them to let you have a taste. Just that small sample can satisfy your craving for sweet/savory in an instant.

- **Split meals** with yourself OR your dining mates. I have seen this work out perfectly so many times. I think we can all agree that restaurant portion sizes are often double or triple what we should EVER eat in one setting. By sharing with a friend/family member, you ensure that you are not feeling forced to continue shoveling food in your mouth when already full. If you and a friend/family member cannot agree on an item to share or you would rather not consider someone else in your meal selection, order your entree with a to-go container. When your meal comes, tuck half of it away immediately and voila, you've got leftovers and you are eating a more reasonable portion of food. Some restaurants also serve lunch or half sized meals for this very reason. Take advantage of that option as well.

- **Eat before you go out.** If you are consistently meal planning, you very well may have already prepared a delicious, healthy meal at home. If so, eat it. Then, when you dine with friends, you can limit your intake to drinks, a light appetizer or maybe even a dessert. The same can be said for filling up on tons of water. We all know the benefits of water, so having a little more than your normal share can help you avoid overindulging when out with loved ones.

Hopefully these tips have provided you with some solid options for enjoying social eating without ruining your healthy eating efforts. The bottom line is: social eating is and always will be a huge part of life. It should be enjoyed with minimal restrictions and no regrets.

Part Two: Exercise

Chapter 4: How to Plan, Prepare and Schedule Workouts

While eating will always be the primary component to losing and even maintaining weight, exercise is STILL extremely important. Not *just* for weight management or the aesthetic piece of looking good from increased muscle definition, but exercise is a NECESSARY component of good health. There are tons of studies and research to support this but here is a quick synopsis of what regular, consistent exercise does for the body:
- Promotes adequate blood circulation
- Improves integrity of cardiovascular system
- Increases overall strength
- Enhances overall flexibility
- Decreases swelling and edema
- Encourages adequate digestion
- Lessens the physical effects of illness
- Facilitates faster healing from injury
- Increases lung capacity and blood oxygenation
- Much, much more

Now that we are on the same page about why it is necessary to exercise, let's figure out how to MAKE TIME for it. "Making" time is clearly just a figure of speech. Obviously, we cannot create time but we can use what we already have more efficiently.

As a busy wife, mom of three and business owner, I get it. There are never enough hours in the day to do what we WANT to do. The reality is though, sometimes our expectations of what we want to fit into a day are unrealistic. If we want to achieve ANYTHING, we have to be realistic. We need to be realistic about what is MOST important and realistic about the demands that we place on ourselves as well as those that we allow others to place on us. I encourage community volunteerism, helping others when you can, facilitating sports/activity participation for your children and supporting the dreams and aspirations of your loved ones. However, I DO NOT encourage doing ALL of the above, at the same time, while consequently neglecting your own self-care. We have all heard it before…you cannot pour from an empty cup. If you do not prioritize yourself FIRST, you are operating on empty and allowing everyone and everything else in your life drain you. We all have times in our lives when we are doing a bit too much and sacrificing for a greater good, but functioning this way for extended periods of time is completely unhealthy. And no matter how well you are sticking to your daily "macros," you will still be susceptible to stress related diseases, fatigue, anxiety and a host of other negative mental and physical repercussions.

So, do yourself a favor and give yourself a break. Eliminate activities, involvements and obligations that are draining you, not serving you and monopolizing your time. This may mean cutting your children's activities/sports. {Raises eyebrows in response to audible gasping from devoted soccer moms} Yes, I said it…or typed it. Kids need extracurricular activities, absolutely, but if your two children each have two activities they are actively engaged in at the same time, you could potentially tie up your time for 2-3 hours, four days each week! That is upwards of 12 hours (or more) each week!! Your exercise requirement for the week is ONLY 2.5 hrs… or 30 minutes, five days each week. Just removing one obligation can give you the time you need to fit in your exercise. Your time is precious, so you HAVE to be honest and realistic with yourself regarding what you can do.

Call on your tribe for support where necessary. Your spouse/partner, older children, extended family members, friends, church family, etc. may all be willing and able to help. Accept assistance when needed to prevent over-exerting yourself or skipping your exercise too often. Outsource things when you can. Consider a weekly, bi-weekly or monthly cleaning service to help keep your home looking nice. Look into a laundry service to free up your time on that chore. Arrange alternating play dates with a friend or even swap babysitting services to give each of you a break every other week. Whatever you need to do to be intentional about taking care of yourself, JUST DO IT.

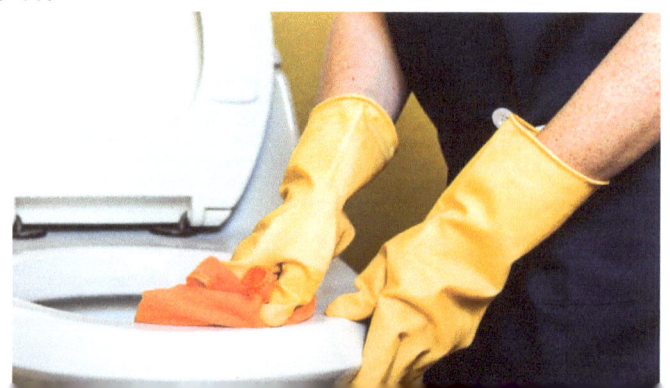

Not only must we be realistic, we need to visually SEE our day/week/month and map out exactly when/where/how we can make time for our workouts (see note in Preface regarding a paper planner). Scheduling your priorities seals them as priorities. Carving out the time in your day gives everything a place and makes you more intentional about doing the things you set out to do. Writing things down in a paper planner is my preference, but this can obviously be done electronically as well. The idea is to plan.

Decide if you are a morning person or if you have more energy in the evenings after work and getting your tasks for the day completed. If you think mornings are most feasible, determine how much time your morning routine takes (without excessive rushing) and tack on an additional 35 minute to get your workout in. If you want to try evenings, determine what time you can squeeze in a 30-minute workout before bed.

Home workouts can be efficient, quick and easy. YouTube has a broad selection of free workouts available. But if you want something more focused and targeted, consider a program that you can purchase, like the 15 Days of Phitness wellness plan.

The 15 Days of Phitness Program was designed by yours truly to help people with busy lives fit exercise and healthy eating into their hectic lifestyles. The guided workouts are only 15 minutes and the additional exercise requirement is 15 minutes of any cardiovascular activity of choice. Brisk walking, bike riding, dancing, the elliptical and many other options can get the job done. The program also includes 15 easy-to-follow recipes, snack suggestions and virtual consultations with a health coach. The components of the 15 Days of Phitness can almost guarantee your success at sticking to a meal plan and exercising 5 days each week. Go to **www.Healthy-Phit.com/15-days-of-Phitness** for more details.

If you prefer getting out of the house for workouts, consider a low-cost gym membership. There are options as inexpensive as $10/month. There are also ways to be extremely creative right in your backyard or at a local park. If you have the time to work in a drive or walk to the gym in addition to your workout, you are off to a great start! Do some online research and find boot camps, free group fitness classes at local churches or community centers, Yoga, Pilates or even boxing-based and other sport-related exercise classes/programs. There are literally thousands of ways and places to exercise. Just pick a few and get started. Try different things as often as possible. Muscle confusion is great for the body and it keeps the mind from getting bored as well.

Later on, we will discuss specific exercises and techniques to utilize in varying places, but for now, just understand the importance of planning and completing your workouts, 4-5 days each week for 30 minutes. That is truly all you need. Couple that with leading a naturally active lifestyle and you are on your way to optimal fitness, or as we like to call it, "Phitness."

Chapter 5: How to Incorporate Kids Into Your Workout Routine

Whether you decide on working out at home, at the gym or in your neighborhood, there will undoubtedly be times when your kids are with you. If those times happen to be at the gym, then obviously, you opted for a fitness center/gym that offers childcare. Otherwise, you may be like many mothers, struggling to figure out a routine that is somewhat accommodating to your child(ren). If this is your situation, here are some suggestions for you.

Complete 30-minutes of exercise while your kids nap. Depending on the ages you are working with here, this may be tricky. But if you can *plan* in advance, you will be successful. If you are home all day with kids, consider wearing your workout clothes and have your preferred workout loaded and ready to go on your phone, computer or memorized in your head. This way, as SOON as you get your munchkins down for a quick nap, hit the play button and get it in! As I mentioned, I have three small children so I am fully aware of the fact that this *plan* will be altered forcibly sometimes, but that is okay. Do what you can when you can and do not stress when your little one awakens early and interrupts your flow. If you can, keep going. I cannot stress enough how important it is for children to see their parents (especially mothers) exercising and leading healthy, active lifestyles. You never know, your child may enjoy watching your sun salutations or cha cha dance moves. And if they are old enough, maybe they will join in.

Speaking of joining in, that is my next suggestion. **Workout WITH your kids.** There are many ways to accomplish this. If you have an infant or small child, consider a 'Mommy and Me' workout like this one I co-starred in a few years ago when my youngest was just 7 months old.

Mommy N Me Workout by Core Elevation Fitness. Available at coreelevationfitness.com

This workout contains all the basic foundational moves to help build core strength and flexibility while simultaneously keeping your baby entertained. There are tons of short workouts like this on YouTube but if you would like great video quality with exercises designed by licensed physical therapists (one of which is also a certified personal trainer), then you will want to try out my suggestion first.

Sometimes, no matter how well your children are behaving, a focused, private workout is what you need. In those cases, **go to the gym.** Many fitness centers have child care as we discussed earlier, but even if yours does not, utilize your local family, friends or neighbors that you trust to watch your "Littles" for an hour. For some of us, just leaving the house and being surrounded by other people working out is super motivational. If you need that, then get that. With this particular suggestion, "incorporating your kids" means setting them up with an activity (playdate, family visit, structured activity at the gym, etc.) while you take the time you need for yourself. Do not let that "mom guilt" take you hostage. You are a better and more well-rounded mother (wife and PERSON) when you are meeting your own needs first. And physical activity/exercise is an actual NEED...though we often treat it like a WANT, but we will talk more about that later.

Often, as busy mothers, wives, caretakers, business women, entrepreneurs, we feel like our needs conflict too much with our children's. If your kids are extremely active and you find yourself toting them around to THEIR sports activities all week long, you are going to have to engage in some extreme multitasking in an attempt to **exercise during your child's sporting activities.** I am sure that this option may cause many of you to pause, but I want to encourage you to keep an open mind about this one. Picture it, your son is out on the field practicing for track and instead of sitting on the bleachers, you walk over to a grassy area and start running laps, doing your own track drills, doing some jumping jacks or even knocking out some burpees. Now, you may feel a bit out of place if you find that all of the other parents are on the bleachers, cool, calm and relaxed. But let's keep in mind that standing out is a good thing, especially in this situation. By taking such a bold stand to put yourself first, you will likely inspire others to follow suit. Who knows, you might start hosting a parent workout during every practice, game or meet that your child has.

It may seem tough, but it is an amazing way to maximize your time. If you feel uncomfortable creating a routine to follow, utilize YouTube or do an easy Google search to give yourself some ideas. Or, try this simple circuit below:
- 100 Jumping Jacks
- 50 Squats
- High Knees (1 min)
- 25 Alternating Forward Lunges
- Alternating Front Kicks (1 min)
- Butt Kicks (1 min)
- 25 Alternating Backward Lunges
- 25 Alternating Lateral Lunges
- Faux Jumping Rope (1 min)
- 25 Burpees

100 Jumping Jacks

50 Squats

High Knees (1 min)

25 Alternating Forward Lunges

25 Alternating Front Kicks (1 min)

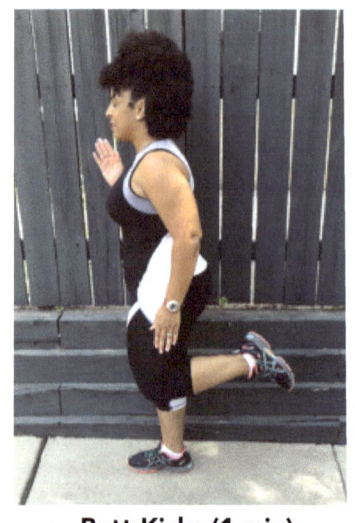
Butt Kicks (1 min)

25 Alternating Backward Lunges

25 Alternating Lateral Lunges   **Faux Jumping Rope (1 min)**

25 Burpees

Repeat twice and you will have completed a pretty effective ~20 minutes of calorie burning and strength training. That will even give you some time to go back and finish watching your kid's practice or game. They will not even have the opportunity to miss you.

Maybe your kids are still small and do not have much going on in the way of extracurricular activities (enjoy it while it lasts). If so, getting them out of the house is still a must and the pressure to ensure they are having a fun and enjoyable childhood can be quite overwhelming. Things like a simple playground trip might seem overwhelming or exhausting if you feel the need to chase after them, ride the slide behind them or push them on the swings for 20 min. I would suggest that you begin to view these things as an opportunity to squeeze in a 15-20 min (or more) workout by **using play time as a workout.** Suck those abs in, adjust your posture and maximize your burn while you enjoy your kids.

A good sweat is a good sweat, right? Well, for those of you that disagree, might I suggest a more structured routine to follow through at the playground? If this interests you, keep reading. I have provided some simple moves that you can adapt to almost any playground setting. The overwhelming point here, though, is to MAKE TIME and KEEP MOVING. When something is an actual priority to you (as your health should be), then you will make arrangements, make plans, make adjustments, make resolutions and make SURE that exercising your body (and eating well) takes precedent in your life. You will begin to fashion your other tasks and habits AROUND your workouts. This process requires a significant amount of maturity and foresight, but with hard work, it can be achieved.

Chapter 6: How to Plan a Workout at the Playground

At first glance, the playground might seem like a dry wasteland as it relates to exercising for adults, but please, take a second look. You might be surprised at the opportunities before you. I am going to highlight popular playground equipment and give a few tips about what each can be used for. As with any exercise routine you are trying to design, it is always a great option to have decided on a target (body area and/or conditioning type). Consider if this will be a cardio workout or a strength training routine. Maybe it will be a combination of both? Whatever you decide to do, write it down (or store it in your phone) and stick to it. Mix it up each time to keep it fresh and fun...and if you are good at persuasion, convince a friend to join you. Consider it a double duty social encounter...one-part play date, one-part team workout.

Let us start with a piece of equipment well known to all of us...the **slide.** Consider any of the following activities in repetition (10-20) to get a good full body burn.
- Walk UP the slide
- Jump off of the edge of the slide
- Jump from the ground to the edge of the slide
- Alternate toe taps from the ground to the edge of the slide
- Run UP the slide
- Run DOWN the slide (carefully)

From the list on previous page, it's clear that just a slide can provide you with a good workout. What about the **monkey bars?** I think it's obvious how easy it would be to incorporate this equipment into a workout but here are some suggestions that you can perform in 30-60 second intervals with 15-30 second breaks in between.
- Hanging from the bars
- Hanging shoulder shrugs from the bars (hanging with a "mini" pull-up)
- Pull-ups
- Climbing UP or DOWN the bars (for dome shaped monkey bars)
- Climbing ACROSS the bars (for linear shaped monkey bars)

The bars can require some serious upper body strength, so remember to mix these moves in with other options. Maybe transition to some core focused exercises using the **swings**. Double check the weight restrictions on swings (and all playground equipment for that matter) so that you are sure not to break anything...or more importantly, hurt yourself. If you are all clear, try the following swing-based moves for up to 15 reps each:
- Planks (feet on swings)
- Tucks (from plank position, bringing feet on swing into body)
- Push-ups (feet on swing)
- Elevated Bridges (feet on swing, back on ground)
- Camel (sitting on knees on ground; arms on swing leaning body forward, then pulling body back to starting position)

Most playgrounds have some **steps** leading up to the slide or other structure. If not, then there is always a nearby curb. Shifting the focus to the legs, try some of these simple exercises for up to one minute each:
- Alternating Running Toe Taps (from the ground to the step)
- Elevated Posterior Lunges (from step to ground)
- Side stepping Up and Down the stairs
- Running Up and Down [skipping] steps

Even if the children's equipment is unavailable for you (too crowded or not necessarily safe for your size), most play areas

have a bench for parents to sit on. You would be surprised at the burn you can get from a **park bench.** Try these exercises:
- Sit to stands at edge of bench seat
- Squat hops (jumping from ground to bench seat and back down)
- Step-ups (from ground to bench seat)
- Incline Mountain Climbers (arms on back of bench, running legs in place on ground)

If you are not fortunate enough to have a fully stocked playground at your disposal or if your playground happens to be over crowded, you can try the circuit suggested for completion during your child's sporting events. If you prefer something with a little less impact, you can do a brisk walk around the play area perimeter for 20 min, march in place or do multiple reps of squats.

The takeaway is that there are tons of ways to utilize whatever you have at your disposal to get in a GREAT workout that is effective, fun and exciting. By switching up your routine regularly, you create a sort of muscle confusion that keeps your body from plateauing and keeps you from becoming complacent.

Multitasking during your children's activities can be tough, so take breaks when you feel like it. That way you can take some time to actually play and engage with your child during their free play. But never feel guilty for focusing on yourself. Your kids are watching you and whether they can understand it now or not, they will be impressed by your efforts. You are setting an amazing example for their future as it relates to valuing health and wellness and ALWAYS taking care of your needs. Whether you are doing a workout, playing on your phone, meditating silently or watching their every move with gratefulness, you are doing what YOU need to do…and that is absolutely vital.

Chapter 7: How to Incorporate Fitness into Your Family Life/Activities

If you are a human living in this present day, chances are you are busy. But if you are a woman, then busy is probably an understatement. Do not then add a career and/or business into the mix. That is enough for anyone to manage, right? But adding a spouse and children, you can likely expect that your fitness routine will suffer greatly. But should it?

The short answer to that question is no, but the effort to ensure that it does not actually happen requires a bit lengthier explanation. I advocate for carving time out of your life for exercise, prayer/meditation, time alone, time with friends, time with your spouse, time with your kids, time with your family, time volunteering, time sleeping, etc., etc., etc. But what happens when there actually is NO TIME??? Perhaps we give up and retreat to the couch to binge watch television and eat snacks? Sure, go ahead. That can be a form of self-care...for a very short season...like a day or two. Ultimately though, we need to take a moment to re-evaluate our goals and our plan of action. Maybe we realize that exercising 45-60 minutes, six days each week is requiring more effort than we can continue to maintain. There is also a possibility that meal prepping for 5-6 hours each week is entirely too time consuming at the

moment. What if we are in a season of life where an ill family member needs our help? What if we are adjusting to a new baby or living through a home renovation?
There are literally MILLIONS of reasons why our "ideal life schedule" may be interrupted for a time (or forever). It is our job in those times to be-
come exceptionally flexible. And I am not just talking about in your muscles, but in your brain. Become flexible in the ideas and plans that your brain has made. You have to be willing to be inconvenienced *and* to work through it to come up with a better solution for the time being. It may be during this time that your separate workouts decrease to twice per week and you find yourself working out with your kids or in an unorthodox setting 1-2 times per week. Maybe you meal prep meals that are more simple and take less time. Frozen vegetables are *still* vegetables. Whatever accommodations you have to make in order to meet the needs of yourself and your family, make them and feel no guilt about it.

A simple way to coordinate more exercise into your life (and your family's) is to allow family time to double as exercise time. Rather than planning a family movie night, consider a family bike ride. Pick a nice, safe trail and roll out together. You can race each other for some sport or make it a leisurely ride along a shaded greenway. This activity can last an hour or more and when you return home, you will have most definitely worked up a sweat. That is family bonding and calorie burning all in one setting.

The list of family fun, heart pumping activities can be pretty exhaustive but here are a few to get you started:
- Attend a workout class as a family
- Go for a family hike on your nearest mountain
- Go roller skating or ice skating together
- Try rollerblading together at a local park

- Go for a family walk/jog in the neighborhood; sprint racing throughout is recommended
- Swim a few laps together in your community pool
- Go rock climbing as a family
- Laser tag war for a sure sweat
- Paintball outing if you can stand the force from those paintballs
- Jump for an hour at a trampoline park
- Take a cardio dance class together (if you can get the men/boys in your family on board)

Whatever you can do that will bring your family closer together and ensure a solid workout, go for it. It is not the first time (and will not be the last) that a woman/wife/mother has had to multitask to meet daily goals. Our entire lives are attempted balancing acts on a tightrope. It takes real effort to pull it off successfully. The beauty is that there is always a net beneath us. When you fall down, you get to get back up and try again.

Chapter 8: How to Navigate the Equipment at the Gym for an Effective Workout

Let us take our fitness back to the gym for a moment. There are many women that make time to get to the gym a few days each week. Whether it is before or after work or early Saturday morning, taking that time to get out of your house and into the gym setting can help you refocus on your fitness goals. There are many days when I crave an uninterrupted workout session to avoid being climbed on by my three-year-old or disturbed by the needs of my five and seven-year-olds. I mean, they are beautiful, sweet little people but constantly pressing pause on my home workouts to help someone to the bathroom or break up a kid fight can be quite annoying and little inefficient.

To reclaim your time at the gym, you need to be able to navigate the equipment seamlessly. All fitness facilities are different, but most have a few key pieces of equipment in common. For the purpose of this chapter, we will focus on those and discuss strengthening specific muscle groups in general.

Let's start at the beginning. If you are headed to the gym, of course it is a great idea to decide what you are planning to work. For example, is this leg day or chest/arms? Maybe today your focus is cardio mostly? Whatever your plan, as long as you have one, you are good. Deciding what you want to do in advance can keep you from wasting your time and energy strolling around the gym. If you are like many women/wives/moms, you have a limited amount of time to spare anyway, so you will want to make the most of it.

Cardio, which is actually short for "cardiovascular" exercise, is a favorite among many, so we will begin our gym journey there. The major benefit of cardiovascular exercise is to support (you guessed it) the cardiovascular system...which includes the heart, lungs and blood vessels. Simply put, this type of exercise keeps the heart pumping sufficiently (after all, it *is* a muscle), the lungs filling and emptying appropriately and all of the blood vessels pushing blood along and breaking down plaque that could potentially clog them up. Cardio is essential to any good workout routine and some of the options typically available at the gym for addressing this are:

- **Treadmill** - everyone's favorite, right? Plan to linger on here anywhere between 10-45 min depending on your distance goal and speed. Treadmills can be used for sprint or distance training. Make sure your footwear is good. Although treadmills are less damaging to the feet/ankles/knees than concrete, there is still quite a bit of force transferring from the load of your body weight. Good shoes with custom orthotics can literally save your feet (knees, ankles and back as well).

At our practice, we exclusively use Sole Supports ™ for custom designed orthotics. Their products are impeccable and fitting is simple, pain-free and effective. Check our their website at www.solesupports.com to find a local provider near you.

- **Elliptical**- This is probably the second most popular piece of cardio equipment at the gym. Utilizing arms and legs (arms are optional), this machine really gives you a full-body burn *without* significantly loading your joints (feet, ankles, knees and hips). Because there is virtually no increased load on the lower body joints, I often recommend the elliptical as a great starting point for someone looking to improve their cardiovascular fitness and/or to begin working toward a large weight loss goal. It is a fairly safe way to burn calories without increasing injury risk.

- **Upright Bike** - The upright bike is another way to really burn those legs and blast those calories with hardly any unnecessary load on your legs. Set a good resistance and pedal away for 20-30 minutes or longer (based on your goals). The only potential downside to the upright bike is the upper back posture that may eventually lead to pain/dysfunction. A bike rider often has his or her upper back flexed (or bent forward) excessively which can cause postural abnormalities (ex: hunchback) and pain later. Be careful to take what I call "extension breaks" (stretching the upper back posteriorly by arching it, leading your eyes up to the ceiling) before, after and during this type of exercise.

- **Seated Bike** - If available at your gym, this machine is ideal for someone with limited endurance in standing or recovering from a lower body injury/surgery such as a knee replacement, ankle sprain or even plantar fasciitis. Being able to sit with support and still get a good cardio burn is priceless. You may find that you have to perform this activity a bit longer and even faster to get a good burn, but it will definitely be worth it. Much like the upright bike, you do want to consider your posture on this bike. This time, focus more on your low back. Be sure that the seat is positioned in a way that provides you with support in the lower or lumbar portion of your back. There is no shame in taking a lumbar roll along with you if necessary. Do whatever you can do to maintain the normal alignment of your spine.

This McKenzie® lumbar roll is our go-to for optimal spinal support in sitting. The strap allows you to take it from your office chair to your car seat and make sure it stays in place. Snag one of these through any major online retailer.

- **Stairmaster** - This option may not be as widely accessible but when and if it is, consider yourself blessed with the ability to workout for a very short period of time while burning calories like you are on a 10-mile hike! Stair masters are essentially walking UP stairs over and over again with *resistance*. Can you even imagine? It does not take long for this one to get your heart pumping and your brow sweating. Just remember, watch your posture and make sure your calves have been stretched out nicely before and after you embark upon this particular workout. If anything in the gym can guarantee you a "Charlie horse," it is this one.

- **Vertical Climber** - If you are not big into fitness, chances are you have never even heard of this particular piece of equipment. It is still fairly new on the scene. But if you ever get the opportunity to try one, I HIGHLY recommend it. The calorie burn on one of these babies is better than all of the aforementioned cardio equipment combined (in most cases). Picture yourself quickly climbing a mountain and that should give you an idea of how this equipment works. Plan to spend about 15 minutes on this machine because much more than that could possibly leave you unable to walk to your car.

Cardiovascular exercise is very important for everyone. Mixing it into your workouts or doing it as one long routine is fine. Ideally, if you are looking ONLY to train your cardiovascular (CV) system and improve endurance, you will want to try to keep your heart rate in the "CV range," which is approximately 220 - your age X .6 through 220 - your age X .7. For example, if you are 36 years old, 220 - 36 = 184. 184 X .6 = 110.4 and

184 X .7 = 128.8. Therefore, when training your CV system, it is most ideal to keep your heart rate between 110-129 BPM (beats per minute). Most cardio equipment will have a way for you to monitor your heart rate and of course, there are tons of fitness/sports watches and even apps on your phone that you can utilize as well. Whether you monitor or not, getting in around 60 minutes of cardio each week is a great practice.

Though many people have a preference between cardio and strengthening, the truth is, you need BOTH in order to sustain all of your body's muscles and systems most thoroughly. Let's look at the machines at the gym that focus on strengthening, starting first, with the upper body. We will include machines that target arms, chest and upper back. For the purpose of this synopsis, we will omit abdominals...simply because most gym equipment is inadequate when it comes to strengthening your abdominals and the rest of your core. In the next chapter we will focus on body weight activities to perform at home to target your abs and core. Also, despite my heavy preference for free weights, we will not discuss them now as the purpose here is to help you become more comfortable with the machines that can sometimes be a bit intimidating. Here are a few common machines that I like for the upper body at most gyms:

- **Bench Press** - This is one of the most misused "machines" at the gym (although in many gyms it may not even be a machine). The most important aspect of the bench press is posture. Make sure the bench height is appropriate for you. When lying down on your back, your knees should be bent to approximately 90 degrees with both feet touching the floor. Your abdominals need to be braced (pulled in tight) and your low back should maintain contact with the bench. Arching the low back puts significant strain on those muscles and can be the cause of much pain later on.

- **Lat Pull Down** - This exercise is often part of a larger unit with cables, rectangular weights, benches and seats for varying exercises. For this particular machine though, there will usually be a wide grip metal bar and a bench to sit on. As with the bench press, you want the bench sitting at an appropriate height for you so that your feet are able to touch the floor when sitting upright. You also need to assume upright posture with a neutral spine. Lat pull downs (which work a large muscle called the Latissimus Dorsi, running along the outer edges of the spine up to the shoulder girdle) should be performed by pulling the bar down IN FRONT OF YOUR CHEST. Sometimes people pull the bar down behind their neck, but this is problematic as it strains the shoulders and may cause injury to the neck. Also, when returning the weight to their original position, control must be exerted to do so without slamming the weights down. Without control, a strong pulling force is placed on the shoulders and injuries may occur.

- **Cable Triceps Bar** - The cables can be a great option, not just for the triceps, but for almost any muscle in the upper body. A simple repositioning of the cables can change a tricep pushdown to a bicep curl. The key with the cables is to make sure you are adjusting the cable to the correct height. For example, with tricep pushdowns, you will want to ensure the height is adequate to allow for your elbows to begin in a position of more than 90 degrees of flexion (bending). Be sure to maintain a nice, upright spinal posture and use your arms ONLY to complete the motion...not the force of your trunk leaning forward and backward.

With all of the equipment at the gym, picking the appropriate amount of weight is of primary importance. I always suggest erring on the side of caution. Try 5-10 lbs. LESS than what you THINK you can handle. If you are able to do a few repetitions with little to no burn, step it up by 5-10 lbs. and go from there. It is vital to find the weight and reps that will both challenge and reward you. Unless you are trying to determine your one rep max, the goal should not be to burnout or pass out.

The same goes for working the muscles of the lower body. There is no shortage of lower body equipment at the gym, but if I am being completely transparent (and true to myself), I do not necessarily recommend any of them. At least, not for most people. I think that machines like the **leg press** and **seated knee extension** can serve bodybuilders and weight lifting competitors well when they are hoping to achieve extraordinary muscle definition. However, these machines and many others (like the **hip abduction/adduction** and the **loaded calf raise**) can do more harm than good. I am sure some of you are clutching your gym bags right now, but it is a hard, cold truth that not many are willing to tell.

The fact is, most of these machines are antiquated and insufficient at best and dangerous at worst. Let's look at them in greater detail for a full understanding of why I am suggesting that you AVOID THE FOLLOWING MACHINES AT THE GYM:

- **Seated leg extension** - This machine probably seems harmless and for most people it is because the weight being used is not significant enough to cause any real damage. But for those who load the machine up with enough weight to require some struggle, may I suggest that the quadriceps (muscles on the front of the thigh that extend or straighten the knee) were never meant to push heavy loads from this seated position. Also, placing too much torque on the lower leg can cause significant pain and damage to the knee...which already handles a lot of load just from the daily requirement of carrying your body weight. Do yourself a favor and skip this machine.

- **Leg Press** - This was a crowd favorite when I would join my dad at the gym he managed back in high school. Nothing makes you feel stronger than pushing the crap out of some weight on a plate. But again, our bodies were not necessarily created to perform such a motion, at least not with such excessive forces of weight. Applying pressure to the legs like that, while lying down is kind of silly. Your legs carry you around all day, so to effect any level of change, you would need to load the machine with more than your body weight. For many people, that amount of weight will cause the lower back to lift off of the machine, redirecting the force of pushing from the buttocks and legs (as intended) to the spine and THAT. IS. NOT. OKAY. Make this machine another one you scoot right past.

• **Hip Abduction/Adduction** - No lie, this machine makes me laugh. Every time I see it, I giggle inside because in my mind I am picturing all the Instagram videos of women in booty-enhancing leggings using this machine in a ridiculous and overly sexual way. The only muscle that gets a great workout from this machine is your IT Band (along the outer edge of your thigh from hip to knee). Since this muscle (which is only partly muscle but mostly connective tissue) is already tight in most people, working it more might have damaging effects on the knee, potentially displacing the knee cap (patella). This machine is an oxymoron in that you are trying to contract and work muscles that you are SITTING on. Unless you are unable to stand, you can ignore this machine. My suggestion, just go ahead and have sex with someone...you will get a more enjoyable hip burning experience.

- **Loaded Calf Raise** - I understand what the creators of this machine were going for. Load the calves with more than your body weight and go to town pumping those ankles up and down. The problem though, is the fact that the weight or load is being dispersed first through the shoulders. Depending on how much weight is chosen, that can have very damning effects on the shoulder girdle itself and also the spine. Gravity gives us enough compression in the spine, we do not need to add more. The shoulder is a complicated, complex and fragile structure, so applying a downward force from weight is not the best idea. Tiptoe past this machine too.

What is left after that? As it relates to lower body exercise machines, not much. There is honestly not one machine that I recommend to work your butt, thighs or calves. I truly believe the most effective and least dangerous way to address these areas is through body weight exercises...all of which CAN be done in the gym, but also, right in the comfort of your home. Good old-fashioned squats, lunges and burpees, coupled with some more advanced moves, like bear crawls, mountain climbers and gorilla hops will get the job done. Adding weights (in your hands) and making your exercises more compound (working the legs AND arms simultaneously) will intensify the moves, improve your overall calorie burn and increase your lower body strength quickly and efficiently.

Chapter 9: How to Design a Workout Without Equipment

Having access to cardio equipment, gym machines, free weights, Yoga mats, BOSUs and other popular exercise materials can be very beneficial. However, NONE of these items are necessary to obtain the wonderful benefits of a great workout. This may seem like a foreign concept to many, but take it from me...someone who does more than HALF of their workouts without any supplies, at home. You absolutely CAN have a powerful and impactful workout utilizing nothing more than your own body weight.

Body weight exercises have been an important part of training the body's muscles since the beginning of time. Before weights and machines existed, lifting, pulling, carrying and raising parts of the body was basically the only component to a good workout. And still today, they add a significant benefit to your fitness program. When would a total body weight workout program be necessary? Perhaps if you are staying in an older hotel without a fitness center...or maybe you have limited space in your home or apartment? What if you are camping or working long days/nights and have absolutely no time for the gym? It is a fact that some people do not want to invest in varying sized weights, elastic bands, kettlebells and the like. With body weight exercises, that is perfectly fine.

When designing an equipment-free workout, it is a good idea to determine what part of the body you are going to focus on, however, it is not particularly necessary. Most times, a thorough equipment-free routine will automatically target many major muscle groups and most importantly, the core. You may want to be sure to organize your exercises in a way that ensures certain parts of your body have "breaks" as the goal is not to burn out any muscle group. I am notorious for 30-minute full-body workouts. They give you the best bang for your time. Below is a sample workout for you to perform without any equipment. Each exercise is performed for 30-45 seconds, followed by a 15-30 second break (depending on your fitness level). Repeat the circuit twice. Begin with a 3-5-minute warm-up of some combination of walking in place, jumping jacks, running in place, jump ropes, or low front kicks. Then, proceed with the following:

- **Mountain Climbers** - From a straight arm plank position, alternate running legs forward toward the hands
- **Squats** - In wide standing with weight in heels, bend both knees keeping the trunk tall and upright
- **Crab Kicks** - From reverse tabletop (weight on hands and feet, front of body facing ceiling), alternate kicking legs reaching opposite hand to toe

- **Alternating Lunges** - In standing, take a large step forward bending the knees to 90 degrees, maintaining an upright trunk
- **Quadruped Alternating Arms & Legs** - From tabletop position (on hands & knees), reach one arm forward while the opposite leg reaches backward; hold then repeat on opposite leg/arm
- **Side Plank Rotations** - From side-lying, lift body up bearing weight on forearm or hand and the side of one or both feet; raise the opposite arm into the air and rotate body reaching the arm under the trunk and return to starting position
- **Tricep Dips** - From reverse tabletop with buttocks lifted off of the floor, bend elbows lowering buttocks toward the floor but not touching; straighten both arms lifting buttocks using triceps and repeat
- **Push-Ups** - From stomach lying position, lift your body weight up using hands/arms and feet, alternately straightening and bending your elbows
- **Alternating Side Kicks** - In wide standing with core muscles contracted, alternate kicking legs to same side of body
- **Plank Jacks** - From a straight arm plank position with abdominals contracted and feet close together, perform a small "jump" opening the legs wide, then return to narrow. Repeat.

Be sure to end with 3-5 min of stretching all the major muscle groups. For this particular workout, you will want to focus heavily on the chest, arms, hamstrings (back of the thighs) and sides of the trunk. Hold all stretches for 30 seconds and perform on both sides of the body.

This workout is a great foundation for an equipment-free burn, but be sure that you understand your body and your capabilities enough to modify when necessary. It is important to challenge yourself to see real change in your strength and fitness, but it is also absolutely okay to modify or change an exercise if it appears to be too challenging for you to complete. The way I suggest you gauge the need for modification is by trying the exercises as listed first. If you are able to complete an exercise for AT LEAST 20 seconds before you feel tired or unable to go on, then a modification is probably unnecessary. Continue with the exercise and you can expect to get better the more you practice. On the other hand, if you are unable to perform the exercise for 10 seconds, consider trying a slightly less challenging move for the full 30-second interval instead. You will ensure that your body gets the full benefit of exercise without risking injury or pain.

There are tons of modification options for exercises. Here are some suggestions for the workout listed above:

Exercise	Modification
Mountain Climbers	SLOW THE PACE OF THE LEG MOVEMENTS OR PERFORM ON AN INCLINE (WITH HANDS AGAINST A WALL OR BENCH).
Squats	DECREASE THE DEPTH OF THE SQUAT.
Crab Kicks	OMIT REACHING WITH THE ARMS.
Alternating Lunges	DECREASE THE DEPTH OF LUNGES.
Quadruped Alternating Arms &	REACH ALTERNATING ARMS FIRST, THEN ALTERNATING LEGS, RATHER THAN AT THE SAME TIME.
Side Plank Rotations	PERFORM WITH KNEES BENT AND/OR OMIT THE ROTATION.
Tricep Dips	DECREASE THE DEPTH OF DIP.
Push-Ups	PERFORM ON KNEES OR AGAINST A WALL ON AN INCLINE.
Alternating Side Kicks	DECREASE THE HEIGHT OF KICKS.
Plank Jacks	ALTERNATELY STEP EACH LEG IN AND OUT RATHER THAN JUMPING.

The beauty of exercise and fitness in general is that you can make it work for you. There is no need to feel the pressure to perform an exercise with the exact same intensity or on the same level as another person. All you need to do is your very best and you will see positive results.

Chapter 10: How to Focus on Your Fitness Without the Weight of Comparison

One of the most disabling phenomena to a fitness journey is a corrupt mindset that chooses to compare one's progress to another. The old saying "comparison is the thief of joy" could not be more true. I would also argue that it is the thief of success, focus and peace. It steals your success by blinding you to it. You are oblivious to and unaware of your "wins" simply because your focus is on what you have yet to achieve. It steals your focus by distracting your thoughts. It is quite difficult to focus on your plan if all you can think of is what someone else "must be doing" on their journey. It steals your peace by causing these thoughts to consume you. Your mind will not be free, at peace and able to enjoy the moments in your life if you constantly spend time each day fantasizing about how much "better" (insert thinner, happier, prettier, smaller, smarter or stronger) someone else appears to be. You have earned your success. You need your focus. You deserve your peace. So, break the cycle today.

Healthy competition can be helpful in many aspects of life. In sports, for example, it can be the driving force that gets you across that finish line first or the motivation that guarantees you the winning catch. In your daily life though, it can be the catalyst for ruined relationships, depression, anxiety and jealousy/envy. If you struggle with comparison and competition in your fitness life (or your life in general), reframe your sense of competition in your mind. Picture yourself at the starting line of a race with several other women beside you eyeing the number one spot. Just before the gun blazes to send you off, look to your left and your right and notice that each competitor looks like your identical twin. Each and every one of

them is YOU. Set this image in your mind and remember that you are your ONLY competition. The goal is to be better than YOU were yesterday and that is it.

There is nothing wrong with being inspired by someone else's journey. There is nothing wrong with wanting *some* of what you see in others, as long as you are willing to work for it. But there *is* something wrong with being so consumed by what someone else is doing that you are unable to create your own vision. **Your** vision is distinctly unique...unlike anyone else's on this earth. Similar to your fingerprint, your vision and purpose belong ONLY to you. You cannot successfully steal someone else's, just as they cannot steal yours. Apologies if this sounds "preachy" to some, but as a faith-based person, I wholeheartedly believe that each and every one of us was placed here and given many of our life circumstances for a specific reason. That reason is key to unlocking our purpose. And that key opens up the door to our vision and ultimately, our happiness. Establishing or finding your "happy" rests almost completely in finding your purpose. It certainly cannot rest in people, because we have no control over others. Our happiness is our own responsibility.

When you have reasserted yourself as the only source of comparison, you can begin the process of becoming the best possible version of yourself. This process begins with assessing where you are currently and where you see yourself in the future. "The future" can be vague, so it might be helpful to set short and/or long-term goals to clarify and quantify what you hope to achieve. This process can be time consuming, but I have found it extremely beneficial over the years to utilize in every aspect of life…career/education, spirituality, personal development and of course, health/fitness. For the purpose of health and fitness, it is ideal to determine what you hope to attain from beginning or continuing along your fitness journey. Consider the following questions:

- Do you want to weigh less? If so, why exactly? To fit into your clothes, to feel good in a bathing suit or something else?
- Do you want to weigh more? If so, why? To fit into your clothes, to feel better in a bathing suit or something else?
- Do you want to have more strength? For what…weight lifting, managing children or something different?
- Do you want to have more endurance? Why…to chase your kids around or run a marathon?
- Do you want to have better muscle definition? For a fitness competition, to take some nice pictures or something different?
- Do you want to feel better? What is your "better?" Is it less fatigue, decreased pain, more mobility, or something else?

Pondering these questions will help you establish the most important piece of the puzzle to your health and fitness. If you know your "what" or your goals and you can conceptualize your "why" or your underlying reason, then you have designed a sturdy foundation for your exercise and wellness practices to be enjoyable, meaningful, exciting and fulfilling. To dig deeper into your "why," you can define for yourself why certain goals are important. For example, **I want to weigh a little less to decrease the load on my joints that cause pain. I want to be able to exercise and teach classes while my children watch and participate from the sidelines. I want them to SEE just how capable women are of managing businesses, caring for family and STILL keeping their own needs at the forefront.** That is a well thought out goal with clear underlying reasons. Qualifying your fitness (or any) goals like this makes them more personal and therefore, more important to conquer.

Getting in better shape should not be a sad, depressing or self-loathing process. You should not feel like you are *fighting* your body or like your mind is detached from the rest of your being. The practical application of positive health and wellness perspectives instills gratitude in oneself for what the body can *already* do and joyful expectancy for what the body *will do*.

Once you are ready to approach your health/fitness goals from this frame of mind, you can attack your goals with tenacity and consistency like never before. From now on, you are not shaming your body into submission or starving yourself to see movement on a scale. Most importantly, you are not idolizing the bodies of people you meet in the gym or envying the lives of your favorite social media influencers. You are hyper-focused on making your journey toward better health, fitness and wellness a POSITIVE experience for yourself and for all those around you. These positive vibes greatly affect those in your circle, including family, friends, co-workers and associates. Imagine the impact on your children's self-esteem when they see their mother truly loving themselves and NOT constantly demeaning themselves. Consider the positive influence on your friends and co-workers when your self-love spills over to them. Recognize the value of loving yourself on this journey, which then gives you the freedom to TRULY love others. Ultimately, that is the goal, right? Love of self and love of others so that we can practice compassion as we seek to be our most well and fit selves. Despite our current position on this never-ending journey, what must stay consistent is the love we have for ourselves, which in turn, fuels our effort to keep moving forward. The more you practice this way of thinking, the more it becomes normal to you. The more normal it becomes, the EASIER your "HEALTHY" is to find.

About the Author

Dr. Lisa Nichole Folden is a licensed physical therapist and the founder of Healthy Phit Physical Therapy & Wellness Consultants in Charlotte, NC. Her physical therapy practice focuses on helping people recover from injury and improve their overall health. As the creator of the #PhitMom Movement, Dr. Lisa works closely with women to help them transition through the varying stages of motherhood. Key aspects of her work involve assisting clients with time management, multitasking, fitness and meal planning and reclaiming the number one position on their priority list.

Dr. Lisa, a native of Detroit, MI and graduate of Grand Valley State University (2004 - B.S., Health Science; 2007 - Doctorate, Physical Therapy), relocated to Charlotte, NC in 2008. Since arriving to Charlotte, she has chaired health & wellness committees, participated in and hosted community events bringing awareness to varying health concerns and presented to hundreds on topics related to health, wellness, fitness and self-care. She is the recipient of several awards for health advocacy and outreach and considers her life's mission to be helping others help themselves.

While managing her private practice, Dr. Lisa also holds the title of wife, to her loving and supportive husband, Darryl and mom to her three amazing children: Aubrey, Addyson and DJ. In her spare time, she enjoys creating fun and creative workouts, crafting with friends and reading all things mystery. With all of the hats that she wears, similar to other mothers/wives/women, Dr. Lisa has made it her personal mission to Make Healthy EASY!

www.ingramcontent.com/pod-product-compliance
Lightning Source LLC
Chambersburg PA
CBHW041626220426
43663CB00001B/30